INBOUND AMPLIFICATION

HOW TO HARNESS PODCASTING

FOR BUSINESS GROWTH

Matt Cheney

Table of Contents

Introduction

It is not easy to get noticed in today's constantly shifting digital environment. Small businesses need more than just a good or service to succeed in the marketplace; they need a platform to share their message. A distinctive tone that connects with its target market, creates memorable brands through engaging narratives, and leaves a lasting impression.

I'm Matt Cheney, a veteran audio professional, content creation coach, and the founder of Kult Media, and I'm here to tell you how content creation and podcasting can be that voice for your business.

With more than 16 years of experience in the media business, including time spent as Vice Media's Head of Audio, I have firsthand knowledge of the transformative power of content. But it was not until I started my first podcast in 2016 that I realised how powerful it could be as a vehicle for engaging listeners, a platform for personal expression, and—most importantly—a cornerstone of an effective inbound marketing strategy.

When I started Kult Media, my goal was to help small businesses, marketing professionals, and creative entrepreneurs navigate the world of content creation. I have witnessed clients' transformations over the years, from being unheard to emerging as thought leaders in their industries. The journey is nothing short of incredible, and I can not wait to take you along for the ride with the help of this book.

Learn the why and how of content creation and podcasting for your small business with this comprehensive guide. We will go over why it is essential to your inbound marketing strategy, how it expands your business and builds your brand, and how to start using it successfully.

With the help of examples and insights from my own and other podcasters journeys, we'll delve into practical steps and strategies. Whether you're just starting out or looking to improve your existing content and podcasting efforts, there's something in here for you.

As we embark on this journey, remember that I'm not just an author imparting information; I'm your coach, here to guide and support you every step of the way.

If you have any questions, please feel free to email me at matt@kult.media While the road may seem daunting, know that with the right direction and the right mindset, it's not only navigable but enjoyable too. After all, business should be serious, but that doesn't mean it can't be fun. So, are you ready to amplify your voice, resonate with your audience, and propel your business to new heights? Let's get started on your content creation and podcasting journey.

Welcome to the first step towards creating a lasting legacy with your brand.

CHAPTER 1

Understanding the Power of Content and Podcasting

The Rise of Content Marketing

In the digital age, traditional forms of outbound advertising and promotion have steadily declined in effectiveness. Modern audiences have grown accustomed to intrusive ads and constant sales pitches. Instead, they crave authenticity, value, and respect from the brands and the people in them vying for their attention.

This gave rise to a new marketing approach called "content marketing." The core strategy is to attract and engage potential customers by creating valuable, relevant content tailored specifically to them.

Unlike constant promotional marketing, content marketing involves providing helpful education, actionable insights, entertaining stories, and solutions to problems the audience cares about. Creating this audience-focused content in formats like blog posts, videos, podcasts, eBooks, and webinars allows companies to build trust and strengthen credibility with readers and viewers.

Content marketing leads cost 61% less than traditional outbound marketing leads (Source: Demand Metric)

 90% of **B2B marketers** use content marketing, up from 78% in 2012 (Source: Content Marketing Institute)

 Businesses that blog receive 97% more links to their website (Source: HubSpot)

 Website visitors who engage with blogs or videos stay on pages over 2.5x longer than non-engaged visitors (Source: LinkedIn)

 93% of marketers say content marketing increased exposure for their business (Source: HubSpot)

 73% of marketers say content marketing efforts increased overall sales (Source: Semrush)

Podcast Marketing Exploded My Website Traffic In 12 Months..... As you consistently appear on industry relevant podcasts, more and more people come to recognise you as a thought leader within the industry, and they seek out your help when they need it. This drives traffic to your website so that they can see what your company does.

Connor Gillivan - FreeeUp [2]

Why Podcasting?

Of the wide variety of content formats and distribution channels, podcasting stands out as one of the most intimate, flexible, and powerful for audience connection.

Over the past ten years, the popularity of smartphones and on-demand audio and video streaming platforms has skyrocketed, catapulting podcasts into the mainstream. According to Edison Research, over 125 million Americans now listen to podcasts on a monthly basis. That's over one-third of the total US population that has made podcasts part of their regular media diet.

1 The number of active podcasts has grown from **300,000** in 2014 to over **4 million** in 2022. (Source: Podcast Insights)

2 Monthly podcast listeners in the U.S. have increased from **75 millionin** 2015 to over **100 million** currently. (Source: Edison Research)

3 Podcast adoption has risen from **9%** of Americans age **12+** in 2008 to 40% in 2022. (Source: Edison Research)

4 Average weekly podcast listening has doubled from **6 hours** in 2014 to over **12 hours** currently. (Source: Edison Research)

5 Globe podcast ad revenue has ballooned from **$479 million** in 2018 to over **$2 billion** in 2022 (Source: IAB)

6 Over **50%** of U.S.households are now monthly podcast listeners (Source: Edison Research)

7 Spotify's podcast audience has tripled from **16 million** in 2019 to over **50 million** currently. (Source: Spotify)

8 Percentage of podcast fans who say they increased podcast listening in the past year: **45%** (Source: Cumulus Media)

Unlike passive forms of content consumption like print or video, the podcast listening experience is intimate and immersive, with the host's voice directly in the listener's ears no matter where they tune in from. This fosters a deep, human connection and relationship between the podcast host and audience over time.

According to a Nielsen survey, 56% of podcast listeners said they were more likely to trust a brand, its goods, or its services after hearing its founder or representatives featured on an interview-style podcast.[3] This reveals the medium's unique power to build brand affinity and loyalty.

Leveraging Podcasting in Your Content Marketing Mix

So what makes podcasting an especially impactful format to incorporate into your overall content marketing mix?

1 **Establishes Thought Leadership and Authority:**

By regularly creating and sharing insightful, educational podcast episodes, hosts cement their status as trusted subject matter experts and authorities.

2 **Builds Meaningful Relationships With Listeners:**

The intimate, immersive audio experience forges powerful emotional connections and relationships between host and audience.

3 **Expands Brand Awareness and Reach:**

With highly shareable episodes and super fans, podcasts continually widen a brand's audience, awareness, and word-of-mouth reach.

4 **Drives Audience Engagement:**

Podcasts facilitate lively engagement and community through participatory tactics like polls, Q&As, discussions, and social media interactions.

5 **Moves Listeners Into Customers:**

By nurturing relationships over many episodes, podcasts can convert engaged listeners into paying customers over time as trust develops.

The Role of Podcasts in Brand Building

In addition to content marketing, podcasts also present a unique opportunity for brands to build identity and shape narrative. Sharing stories, perspectives, insights, and discussions through podcast episodes gives a brand a human voice and personality. This not only generally promotes brand awareness, but more importantly, it allows brands to form authentic emotional bonds by resonating with specific audiences. Podcasts that consistently deliver value to listeners can gain dedicated, loyal communities and followings, solidifying the brand's presence and growth.

The 7-11-4 Principle

Understanding the behaviour of your audience is essential in the world of marketing. One such understanding is encapsulated in the 7-11-4 principle, a concept introduced by Daniel Priestley in his book "Oversubscribed".

This principle is based on the human brain's tendency to form connections based on time, interactions, and locations.
Let's break it down:

..→ 7 Hours: The first part of the principle suggests that spending more than 7 hours with someone transitions them from an acquaintance to a friend. In the context of business, this means that your potential customers should have at least 7 hours of content to engage with.

..→ 11 Interactions: The second part of the principle posits that people with more than 11 interactions with a brand are more likely to buy from that brand. Emails, social media posts, phone calls, and other forms of communication could all be used in these interactions.

..→ 4 Locations: The final part of the principle states that seeing people in different places creates a stronger bond. In the context of marketing, this means that your brand should be present in at least 4 different places or platforms.

Now, how does podcasting fit into this principle? Let's explore.

Podcasting and the 7-11-4 Principle

Podcasting is a powerful tool that can be used to effectively implement the 7-11-4 principle. Here's how:

→ **7 Hours:**   A podcast series can easily provide more than 7 hours of content for your audience to engage with. Each episode can delve into different aspects of your business, industry trends, interviews with experts, or even customer stories. This not only keeps your audience engaged but also positions your brand as a thought leader in your industry.

→ **11 Interactions:**   Each podcast episode can be an interaction point. Moreover, promoting your podcast on social media, sending email newsletters about new episodes, or engaging with listeners in the comments section can all count towards these interactions. Remember, every touchpoint is an opportunity to strengthen the relationship with your audience.

→ **4 Locations:**   Your podcast can be distributed across multiple platforms, such as an email newsletter, your website, Apple Podcasts, Spotify, and Google Podcasts. Additionally, you can leverage social media platforms to promote your podcast episodes. This multi-platform presence not only increases your brand's visibility but also allows your audience to engage with your content in a way that's most convenient for them.

Growing Business and Revenue with Podcasts

With compelling, high-quality content, business podcasts also become powerful engines for tangible business growth and revenue in multiple ways:

- » Generate new website traffic, leads, and newsletter subscribers through clear calls-to-action.

- » Increase conversions and sales by promoting products, services, and specials during episodes.

- » Attract podcast sponsorships and advertisements from relevant brands.

- » Drive product sales through unique promo codes and special offers.

- » Inspire direct listener donations through platforms like Patreon or BuyMeACoffee.

- » Provide "insider" premium content and community access to paying members.

- » Get booked as a guest on other popular podcasts within the industry.

- » Build strategic partnerships and collaborations with mutually aligned brands.

As you can see, podcasting is a great way to build brand awareness, strengthen connections with your audience, and grow your business. In the next few chapters, we will talk about podcasting strategies and how to start your first business podcast.

CHAPTER 2

Podcasting: The Game-Changing Content Marketing Powerhouse

Defining Podcasting

The concept of podcasting first emerged in the early 2000s as enterprising technophiles realised the potential of the newly available MP3 audio format combined with abundant internet bandwidth and storage. They recognised that audio files could be offered as on-demand "episodes" for audiences to download or stream at their convenience—not too different from traditional radio shows but completely flexible and user-controlled.

The term "podcasting" is credited to former MTV VJ Adam Curry, who coined the name as a fusion of Apple's immensely popular iPod device for MP3 playback and "broadcasting." The name stuck as hobbyists and innovators pushed the new medium forward.

VJ Adam Curry

Say hello to iPod.
1,000 songs in your pocket.

By definition, a podcast is an episodic digital audio or video file series. Episodes are available for download or on-demand streaming via the internet or mobile apps for listeners' devices. This flexibility and ease-of-use in when, where, and how to access podcasts make them an incredibly user-friendly, intimate media format.

The Mainstream Explosion of Podcasting

Since its inception just over 15 years ago, podcasting has quickly become popular, largely due to the explosive growth of smartphones, mobile broadband connectivity, and streaming. According to Edison Research, more than 100 million Americans now listen to podcasts on a regular basis. [4] That amounts to more than one-third of the entire US population who regularly consume audio and video content on demand.

In fact, according to HubSpot research, 70% of Americans are now familiar with the concept of podcasting, indicating unmatched mainstream penetration for this once niche digital medium.

The Steady Rise of Podcasts

Percentage and number of Americans (12+) who have listened to a podcast in the past

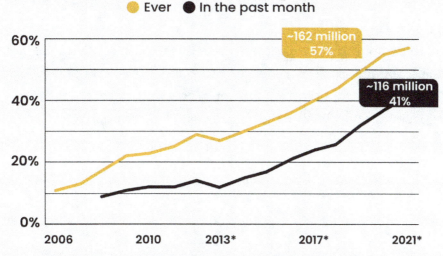

● Ever   ● In the past month

* in 2013, the source changed the definition of what qualifies as a podcast
Sources: Edison Research, Triton Digital

Unique Benefits of Podcasts for Businesses

For companies and entrepreneurs, podcasting offers numerous compelling benefits not found in other forms of content or advertising.

Forging Personal Connections

Unlike passive forms of media consumption like print, video, or even social media scrolling, the podcast listening experience is intimate, with the host's voice literally in the listener's ears no matter where they tune in from. This facilitates a sense of human-to-human connection between host and audience.

55% of regular podcast listeners reported "feeling as if they have a personal connection to the hosts" and viewing them as reliable friends or advisors, according to an impact study by the Pew Research Centre in 2021. [5]

This interpersonal dynamic allows businesses to build relationships that feel genuine and familiar, not merely transactional. Savvy companies invest in high-quality podcast productions not simply for marketing but to nurture this special connection with their customers and community.

Establishing Thought Leadership and Trust

By consistently creating and sharing insightful, educational episodes, businesses can establish authority and cement their status as trusted subject matter experts.

Edison Research found that 66% of Americans who listen to podcasts monthly say they rely on podcasts to provide them with information about topics they care about, indicating they turn to podcast hosts as trusted resources on what matters most. [6]

This gravitas holds immense influence in building brand reputation and affinity. As listeners come to depend on hosts' expertise, they are far more likely to turn to that business when they need related products, services, or solutions.

20

Expanding Brand Reach and Awareness

With highly shareable episodes and vocal fans who evangelise, podcasts offer unparalleled word-of-mouth reach for businesses.

Per Edison Research, roughly one out of every two podcast listeners (48%) has shared about a podcast they love with friends or on social media. This provides exponential exposure beyond just the initial download numbers. [7]

Even smaller startups can rapidly expand brand visibility and recognition through compelling podcast content that gets audiences talking.

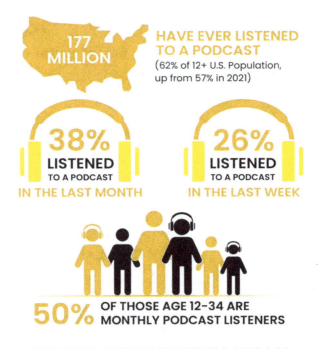

177 MILLION

HAVE EVER LISTENED TO A PODCAST
(62% of 12+ U.S. Population, up from 57% in 2021)

38% LISTENED TO A PODCAST IN THE LAST MONTH

26% LISTENED TO A PODCAST IN THE LAST WEEK

50% OF THOSE AGE 12–34 ARE MONTHLY PODCAST LISTENERS

WEEKLY U.S. PODCAST LISTENERS AVERAGE:

8 PODCAST EPISODES IN THE LAST WEEK

Case Studies of Impactful Brand Podcasts

This powerful medium has delivered impressive real-world results for many companies that integrate it into their marketing strategies.

The Skimm: "Skimm This" Daily News Podcast

» Launched in 2018 as an extension of their popular daily email news curation.

» Provides deeper dives into top headlines and stories.

» increased audiences by 42% in one year, according to Podsights.

Slack: "Variety Pack" Business Podcast

» Showcases diverse perspectives on work culture, leadership, and innovation

» Enhances Slack's brand as a forward-thinking, engaging company

» Boasts a 4.9-star rating on Apple Podcasts with over 2800 glowing reviews.

HubSpot: "The Growth Show" Marketing Podcast

» Established strong thought leadership in inbound marketing and sales

» Helped "massively accelerate" awareness, traffic, and leads, according to the founder.

» Grown to over 200 episodes and 7.5 million downloads since its 2015 debut.

» The Tremendous Content Marketing Potential

This chapter provided an in-depth look at the vast landscape of content creation and its transformative effects on businesses. From articles to videos, and particularly podcasts, we've unearthed the potential each medium holds. But the question lingers: How can we ensure our content, regardless of its form, deeply resonates with our audience? How do we guide them from casual interaction to dedicated loyalty? The answer lies in a methodical approach that transcends the boundaries of content type. In the next chapter, we introduce the K.U.L.T. framework, a versatile strategy that works seamlessly across all content platforms, driving your audience from mere awareness to unwavering brand loyal]ty.

CHAPTER 3

Introducing the K.U.L.T. Framework for Inbound Marketing Success

In the content creation realm, connection is your most potent weapon. Every piece of content, be it a riveting blog, an evocative video, or a captivating podcast episode, serves as an invitation—a beacon for your audience to enter your brand universe. The brilliance of the K.U.L.T. framework is in its orchestration of this audience journey—from a fleeting encounter to an unshakable bond, culminating in their investment. This investment transcends monetary value; it's about garnering their unwavering attention, including them in their daily narratives, and influencing their choices. This chapter provides a comprehensive overview of the K.U.L.T. framework, empowering you with insights to refine your content strategy and leave an indelible mark on your audience.

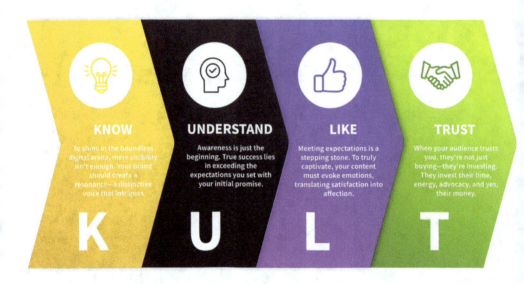

KNOW

To shine in the boundless digital arena, mere visibility isn't enough. Your brand should create a resonance—a distinctive voice that intrigues.

K

UNDERSTAND

Awareness is just the beginning. True success lies in exceeding the expectations you set with your initial promise.

U

LIKE

Meeting expectations is a stepping stone. To truly captivate, your content must evoke emotions, translating satisfaction into affection.

L

TRUST

When your audience trusts you, they're not just buying—they're investing. They invest their time, energy, advocacy, and yes, their money.

T

K = Know

To shine in the boundless digital arena, mere visibility isn't enough. Your brand should create a resonance—a distinctive voice that intrigues listeners. Here, the art of packaging and presentation, combined with engaging hooks, comes into play. They aren't just eye-catchers; they're a promise of the value that lies within.

Strategies and Details:

» **Attention-Grabbing Content:** Craft standout content that resonates using vibrant visuals and compelling narratives relevant to your audience.

» **Consistent Output:** Regularly populate the digital space to reinforce and expand your brand's presence. This does not mean insane volume or low-quality content; consider your brand's value and reputation.

» **Packaging and Presentation:** The allure of your content lies in its presentation—it's a pledge to the viewer of the treasures that await inside. Engaging Hooks: Lure your audience with compelling questions, anecdotes, or intriguing data, promising them a journey of value specifically for them.

Example: An innovative tech brand releases a teaser that's not only visually stunning but also promises groundbreaking features. It hints at the wonders within without revealing everything, fueling audience curiosity. They use colours, images, sounds, and language that speak specifically to their desires or pain points.

U = Understand

Awareness is just the beginning. True success lies in exceeding the expectations you set with your initial promise. It's here that your content should not only deliver but go beyond, creating that enlightening "Aha!" moment. You establish a relationship of value and dependability when you fulfil the promise that your packaging and hooks hint at. Typically, creators look to educate, entertain, and inspire.

Strategies and Details:

» **Educational Content:** Illuminate your offerings through clear and comprehensive content forms, ensuring the audience's promise is more than met.

» **Storytelling:** Use compelling narratives, testimonials, and stories that not only resonate but also reinforce the trust and value you promised.

» **Clear Communication:** Translate your value proposition lucidly, ensuring that the richness inside matches the allure outside.

Example: An eco-friendly brand promises a blend of luxury and sustainability. Their detailed content then showcases not only the opulence and quality of their products but also their genuine commitment to the environment and insight into how they are making a difference in the world, exceeding customer expectations.

L = Like

Meeting expectations is a stepping stone. To truly captivate, your content must evoke emotions, translating satisfaction into affection. When you consistently deliver on promises and kindle emotions, your brand becomes more than a choice—it becomes a part of their personal narratives.

Strategies and Details:

» **Emotion-Driven Content:** Create content that evokes powerful emotions, transitioning audience members from passive consumers to brand ambassadors.

» **Engagement Activities:** Propel active engagement through interactive sessions, transforming satisfaction into genuine brand affinity.

» **Community Building:** Cultivate spaces where followers can share their joy, stories, and feedback, turning positive experiences into shared celebrations.

Example: A boutique bookstore, after promising a curated and personalised reading experience, shares a video series titled "Stories Beyond Pages." Each episode captures the emotional journeys of readers as they rediscover long-lost memories or form new ones, all through the books they've acquired from the store. The heartwarming tales not only highlight the promise delivered but also amplify the emotional resonance of every purchase, making the brand an integral part of their reading rituals and memories.

T = Trust

When your audience trusts you, they're not just buying—they're investing. They invest their time, energy, advocacy, and yes, their money. This trust is cultivated when you consistently honour your promises, exceed expectations, and kindle emotions.

Strategies and Details:

- » **Value-Driven Content:** Uphold the promise of value by delivering consistent and enriching content.

- » **Transparency:** Show the mechanisms behind the magic, reinforcing the trust your audience places in you.

- » **Engage and Respond:** Ensure every query, feedback, or story shared by your audience is acknowledged and celebrated.

- » **Testimonials and Reviews:** Real-life affirmations bolster your brand's commitment to delivering on its promises.

Example: Consider an artisanal coffee brand that differentiates itself with the promise of ethically sourced beans and a commitment to sustainable farming practises. Over time, through engaging content, the brand shares behind-the-scenes footage of the local farmers they partner with, their farming methods, and the community projects they support. This content not only educates customers but also evokes a deep emotional connection. A regular cafe-goer might then choose this brand over others because she believes in its ethos and feels a personal connection with the stories shared

.

One day, she walks into a store and spots two bags of coffee beans: one from a well-known commercial brand and another from this artisanal brand. Even though the latter is slightly more expensive, she chooses it because of the emotional connection and trust the brand has created.

Over the years, her loyalty to this coffee brand has deepened. She subscribes to their monthly delivery, gifts their products to friends, and even visits one of the farms during a vacation. This emotional bond, stemming from shared values and trust, doesn't just translate to a one-time purchase but evolves into a lifelong partnership, amplifying the lifetime value of the customer for the brand.

Key Questions To Ask

When crafting your inbound marketing strategy using the K.U.L.T. framework, it's essential to always ask:

1. Do they know me?

2. Do they understand my value?

3. Do they like my brand's personality?

4. Do they trust me enough to invest?

By addressing each of these questions with the detailed strategies provided, your inbound marketing efforts are poised for success.

With the K.U.L.T. framework meticulously laid out, you have the tools and mindset to revolutionise your inbound marketing endeavours. You've been shown the roadmap to escort your audience from mere awareness through understanding, right up to the altar of trust. While each phase of the K.U.L.T. approach is a powerful force in its own right, its culmination in creating deep-rooted trust provides fertile ground to introduce new mediums and strategies.

However, while written content, visuals, and social media play an undeniable role in inbound marketing, the world of podcasting emerges as a formidable and often under-utilized force. With the ability to establish genuine connections, intimate dialogues, and a sense of community, podcasting stands out as a unique medium that perfectly dovetails with the objectives of inbound marketing.

CHAPTER 4

Integrating Podcasting into Your Inbound Marketing Strategy

Let's dive into how podcasting can powerfully amplify results for inbound marketing, the strategy of earning potential customers' attention through valuable content experiences tailored to them.

What is Inbound Marketing Exactly ?

Inbound marketing developed as a methodology to attract and engage customers online by creating content designed to address their pain points and provide value, rather than interrupting them with traditional outbound advertising and promotional tactics.

Specific inbound strategies include:

» Creating relevant, compelling blogs, videos, podcasts, eBooks, webinars, and other formats that directly help the target audience solve problems and achieve goals This content acts as a "magnet" to pull in ideal visitors when optimised for search.

» Conducting keyword research to understand what potential customers are searching for and optimising all content assets for visibility on SERPs so the right people can easily discover them.

» Engaging audiences on social media platforms through shares, discussions, polls, and relationship-building to foster a sense of community.

» Using clear calls-to-action across all touchpoints to convert strangers into leads, leads into customers, and customers into delighted brand evangelists.

The main objective of inbound marketing is to attract attention by being remarkable, genuine, human, and transparent rather than by buying it.

Unique Benefits of Podcasting for Inbound Marketing Goals

So how can integrating podcasting into the mix amplify results for marketers pursuing inbound strategies?

Establishing Unmatched Thought Leadership and trust

By consistently publishing episodes loaded with insider knowledge, tactical tips, valuable lessons, and subject-matter expertise, hosts quickly establish gravitas and authority in their niche.

Over 80% of monthly podcast listeners say they value the specialised knowledge hosts offer on topics that are important to them, according to a Discover Pods survey. [8]

This cements podcasters as trusted experts that audiences look to for guidance on challenges and goals. Increased affinity and reliance on a brand boost conversions. Because of this, if you do not have the means to start your own podcast, you should seriously consider making appearances as a guest on established podcasts in your field to reap the same benefits but without the investment. However, appearing as a guest on a podcast necessitates inconsistent content creation that lacks your precise brand and narrative.

Forging Powerful Emotional Connections And Relationships With Audiences

The intimate, immersive audio experience forges a personal connection between host and listener, even at scale. After all, the only other voice you usually hear in your head is yourself.

> **Over half of regular podcast listeners say that they feel as though they "know the hosts" personally and regard them as reliable friends, according to an impact study by the Pew Research Centre.** [9]

These powerful emotional bonds drive trust, advocacy, loyalty, and lifelong customers.

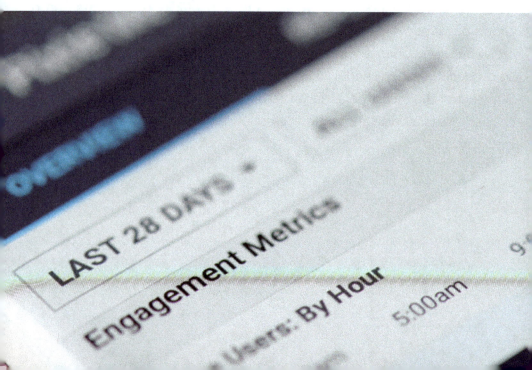

Driving Qualified Traffic to websites

Podcasts drive targeted traffic to hosts' websites by including links in show notes, transcriptions, or podcast directory profiles.

Per the latest benchmark data from the Content Marketing Institute, 48% of podcast listeners have visited a show's website after listening to an episode to explore more. [10]

This traffic can be leveraged with onboarding funnels to generate email subscribers, demo sign-ups, lead generation offer downloads, and more.

Converting Engaged Listeners into customers

Once we have built and earned the trust of our listeners, we can ask them to engage with us on a professional level. Podcasts can include direct response calls-to-action to convert listeners into leads and customers, like limited-time discounts, access to exclusive resources, or free assessments or demos.

As per LeadQuizzes, 65% of B2B marketers surveyed affirmed that their branded business podcast was an effective channel for generating new leads and customers—higher than any other medium. [11]

Facilitating Vibrant Community Building and engagement

Savvy podcasters foster lively communities around their shows via dedicated private discussion forums, interactive social media channels, episode reviews, polls, surveys, and live or virtual events with their audiences.

These digital and offline venues allow listeners to connect with hosts, guest experts, and other fans, fulfilling intrinsic human needs for belonging and esteem.

Execute an Inbound Strategy with Podcasting as a Core channel.

With immense potential for lead generation, brand building, community cultivation, and driving measurable business growth outcomes, podcasting should be leveraged as a foundational channel within holistic inbound marketing strategies.

By this, we mean that podcasts aren't merely another platform for your business to maintain a presence on; they are a springboard for a multitude of other content forms. This idea comes from the fact that podcasts are inherently long-form, which gives you the chance to go deeper into topics, making for richer conversations and more meaningful content.

As a result, a variety of other types of content can be derived from this long-form content. A single podcast episode, for instance, could be repurposed into a collection of social media posts, an in-depth blog post, material for speeches or webinars, or even a new digital product. By using content for multiple purposes, you not only increase your reach across platforms but also contribute to the development of a unified brand story.

CHAPTER 5

Launching Your Business Podcast: A Deep Dive Into Planning, Production, and Promotion

Now that we've explored the marketing superpowers of podcasting, let's do an extensive review of the core logistics of launching your own branded business podcast.

Step 1: Strategic Planning for Maximum Impact

Thoughtful planning is crucial for ensuring your show is set up for long-term success. Here are key considerations:

Your Motivations and Ambitions

Why are you making this podcast, and secondary to this point, why are you the best person to do it? The key to successful inbound marketing is to have clear objectives and goals to act as your guiding light. If you can't get a clear and concise "why" statement, you will struggle to give the content the resources and significance it requires to make it a success.

Establish specific, measurable goals you want to achieve by launching a podcast. Examples: lead generation, brand awareness, establishing thought leadership, driving conversions, etc. These goals will guide decisions from podcast format to release cadence and promotion strategies.

Pinpoint Your Target Audience and Engage them

Define your ideal listener persona in detail, including demographics like age, location, and gender, as well as psychographics like interests, values, and pain points they face. Conduct user interviews and distribute audience surveys if needed to further clarify who you aim to serve. This will directly inform show topics and content style. This task is of paramount importance! I can not stress enough how crucial audience and ideal client market research is to the success or failure of your podcast. In this task, you cannot collect too much information. To maximise the return on investment from your inbound marketing, you must engage your potential audience early and truly comprehend their perspectives.

Choose an Impactful Format Aligned with Your Goals and Desires of Your Ideal Listener

» Solo-hosted shows build intimate personal authority and give you the freedom to share your unique perspective. Example: Podcast Accelerator with Mark Asquith

» Interviews with industry experts allow you to engage prominent thought leaders in your space, providing listeners with value. Example: The Tim Ferriss Show

» Panel discussions encourage debate, rapport, and the sharing of diverse opinions by including multiple hosts and guests. Example: Entrepreneurs on Fire

» Storytelling formats Allow you to share compelling stories that emotionally engage audiences. Example: Dan Carlin's Hardcore History

» Hybrid approaches like mixing interviews, panels, and solo shows

   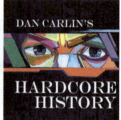

Podcast Accelerator / The Tim Ferriss Show / EO on Fire / Hardcore History

Select Compelling Topics and Outline Content Pillars

Deliver your ideal listener the content they need and want!

Choose recurring topic areas and pillars that align with your brand, expertise, and audience interests and questions. Stick to focused pillars rather than scattering your content across too many unrelated themes.

Outline pillars that will distinguish your show and clearly establish your niche thought leadership position. Examples could include industry commentary, success stories, tactical how-to advice, insider interviews, trend analysis, journalism focused on your field, etc.

Your target audience research should ensure that you never run out of ideas for podcast topics and themes. If you are not able to outline 20 to 30 podcast episodes, go back to the market, find out what they are looking for, and align that with your viewpoint.

Create a Title and Tagline That represent Your Show's essence

Your title should be descriptive, memorable, and communicate the tone and niche of your show. Example: Smart Passive Income, "Daily tips and strategies for becoming financially free through online sources of income."

Title optimisation can be made easier with tools like Google Search Console and ListenNotes.

Do not make your brand and title too hard to understand. They should be easy to find in search engines, even if someone is not looking for a particular podcast. A tagline that summarises the central premise and value proposition helps quickly introduce your show. Example: Where art and entrepreneurship collide. Keep it clear and memorable.

This first step of pre-production is the foundation for your content and inbound marketing strategy. This process deserves an entire book of its own to detail the significance of this step.

It is really tempting to overlook or downplay step 1, but getting these five exercises completed and as thoroughly thought out as possible will set you up for greater success.

Step 2: Key Technical Steps and Tools

This is the step everyone seems to jump to when starting a podcast.

What microphone do I need? How do I record? Do I need video? How do I edit? These are all valid questions, but I must insist that if you have not completed the actions in step 1, the longevity of your content is at serious risk, and thus the production process will not matter if you stop your podcast.

However, if you have completed step 1, let's discuss podcast production. Achieving professional-quality audio is very attainable for non-pros with the right simple gear and software.

Recording Your Podcast Episodes

Your recording space matters more than your microphone. I have used $1,000 microphones and $50 microphones and had better results podcasting with the cheaper microphone. Why? Because the space and the microphone were better suited.

The room you record in will make all the difference to your podcast's sound, rather than the quality of your microphone. So seek to find an acoustically suitable space for your podcast. We want minimal noise, very few shiny reflective surfaces, lots of soft furnishings, and as much comfort as possible (podcasts can take a while, you'll want to be comfy).

Video vs. Audio-only: For ease, an audio-only podcast is the best way to get started. They are easier and cheaper to launch, as well as being far less stressful and more editable than video podcasts. But there are some significant benefits to video, such as greater marketing and content repurposing opportunities.

Injecting video into your content mix adds a little thing called 'production value,' which in layman's terms means money... or expertise.

Production value is the quality of the video you're putting together— the lighting, sound, picture, set, etc. Everything that could potentially make a viewer say, "Wow, this looks so professional" or "Wow! This looks like it was thrown together in five minutes!"

It's important to understand how much work goes into creating video content so you can be realistic about whether you've got the time to churn out a consistently good show.

Rachel Corbett - PodSchool [12]

Now for the microphones, we can't have a podcast without a method of capturing your voice. I recommend you invest in a dynamic USB microphone like the ATR2100 or Shure MV7, which provide studio-quality vocal recording. Expect around a $100–250 initial investment. Both are adequate, but I think that you can't outgrow the MV7 in terms of both sound and build quality.

Audio Technica ATR2100 & Shure MV7

If you want to record multiple contributors, you will want to consider XLR connections to an audio interface. You should not use multiple USB microphones into the same recording device, whether that be a phone, laptop or high powered desktop computer. Don't do it, it will cause errors and headaches.

Use recording software like Garageband (Mac) or Audacity (cross-platform). These options are free to start with. Eventually, upgrade to software like Adobe Audition, Descript, Reaper, or Pro Tools. Alternatively, if you do not want to record into a computer, you can use a recording device such as a Rodecaster Pro, Zoom H6, or even your smartphone.

Rode Rodecaster & Zoom H6n recording devices

If you are doing remote recordings, I recommend Riverside.fm for high-quality video and audio capture over something generic like Google Meet or Zoom.us

This is a super easy way to host and record ... but not free unfortunately.

Riverside.fm remote recording session

For more help in hosting and recording your very first podcast, you can access my Practical Podcasting Checklist to help you set up your podcast like a pro! Head to www.kult.media/checklist to download your free guide.

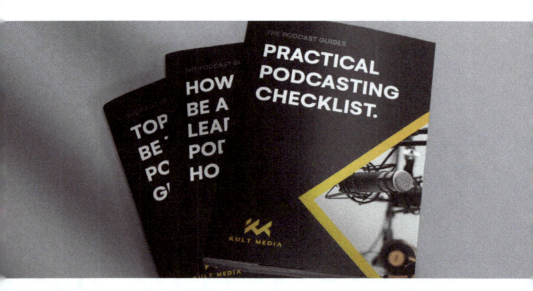

Editing Your Episodes

Do I need to edit my podcast? This is a question I get asked a lot. And the simple answer is yes. You should be curating your listeners' experiences to ensure they get the best possible content. Producing and distributing unedited content might damage your brand's reputation, waste your listeners time, and not provide a return on investment. So I do recommend that you produce all of your content to the highest standard, relevant to your audience and objectives.

Editing software like Descript, Garageband, Audacity, or Adobe Audition. Entry-level options have basic editing capabilities.

Essential editing tasks include noise reduction, removing mistakes, improving vocal tone, balancing sound between speakers, and adding intro and outro music.

Giving your show a structure and improving storytelling are two other important reasons to edit it. Your podcast will benefit from having an engaging structure and format, which will be appreciated by your listeners. This also applies to attempting to keep your show's duration within a certain range. Going from 20 minutes to 3 hours between episodes will cause you to lose listeners.

This is an example of a show structure that I have used on various podcasts:

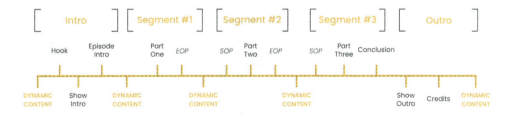

As you can see, a straightforward monologue or interview is divided into sections, allowing for the curation of topics to have the greatest possible impact. In addition, we make room for introductions, justifications, promotions, and calls to action. After the interview, you can complete all of these tasks, saving your guest time.

Hosting and Distribution

A podcast hosting platform is an online service that provides storage, generates RSS feeds, and facilitates the distribution of podcast episodes to various platforms and directories on the internet. It works in a similar way to website hosting, except instead of a URL, we have an RSS feed address.

Use Captivate, Libsyn, Buzzsprout, Omny Studio, or similar hosting platforms ($5–$20/mo) to host your episodes online and distribute them to major podcast platforms. I recommend Captivate because of its ease of use, feature set, and advanced tools to help podcasters market and monetize their shows.

Once your hosting is all set up, submit your podcast feed to directories like Apple Podcasts, Spotify, Google Podcasts, etc. to make your show discoverable across platforms.

Here are the key components and functions of a podcast hosting platform:

» Storage: Platforms for hosting podcasts offer storage space for podcast episodes' audio or video files. The people who make podcasts upload these files, which are then kept safe on the platform's servers.

» Each podcast has its own RSS (Really Simple Syndication) feed, which the hosting platform creates. This feed has important information about the podcast, like the title, description, release date, and link to the media file for each episode. With the RSS feed, podcast platforms and directories can automatically get and show the most recent episodes of the podcast.

» Distribution: Once the podcast is hosted on the platform, the RSS feed makes it possible to send episodes to different podcast directories and platforms, such as Apple Podcasts, Spotify, Google Podcasts, and more.

» Analytics and Statistics: Platforms for hosting podcasts give podcast creators analytics and statistics about how well their podcast is doing. Creators can keep track of how many downloads, listens, and other metrics their episodes get to learn more about their audience and how popular their episodes are.

» Customization: Many hosting platforms let podcast creators change things like the artwork, description, and links to their website or social media.

» Making money: Some hosting platforms have built-in ways to make money from podcasts, such as dynamic ad placement or the ability to offer premium content to subscribers.

» Libraries and Episodes: People who make podcasts can use the platform to organise their episodes and take care of their podcast library. They can schedule episodes, publish or unpublish them, and make changes as needed.

Step 3: Promoting and Growing Your Podcast

A mistake I see time and time again with podcast marketing and content creation is launching first and promoting your podcast after. In step 1, we should be engaging your ideal audience. This is a great opportunity to start the conversation and share the upcoming content you are going to create.

Do not let your launch date be the first time your target audience discovers your content.

Promoting your show early and consistently is crucial to expanding your reach, building engagement, and growing your listener base over time.

Tactics include:

» Sharing new episodes across your website, email lists, and existing social media channels. Make sharing frictionless.

» Ask your existing audience to recommend and share the podcast. Word of mouth is still one of the best forms of marketing. You could incentivize with promotions and competitions to reward your listeners.

» Appear as a podcast guest to gain access to other hosts' audiences. Offer to reciprocate cross-promotion. Collaboration is key in podcasting!

» Run targeted podcast ads on platforms like Overcast, Spotify, and podcast networks to find receptive new listeners. Be wary of doing this without attempting to engage your audience first; it can become costly.

» Build promotional partnerships with relevant brands that can share your show with their aligned audiences.

» Implement SEO best practises like transcripts and shownotes to improve discoverability across podcast platforms.

» Implement SEO best practises like transcripts and shownotes to improve discoverability across podcast platforms.

» Feed Swaps are a great way to network and access other people's podcast audiences. You agree to share other creators' relevant content with your audience, and they will do the same in return, giving the listeners added value and new content.

» Hosting events and meetups. Your content is made for a specific audience; why not bring them all together and build a stronger community? A tactic you can use in the development stage of a podcast is to consider what an event or live version of the podcast might look like, and in doing so, you will consider how to make the show as engaging as possible.

This list is by no means exhaustive, but it can get you moving in the right direction. If you have any questions about audience growth or inbound marketing, please feel free to contact me.

You are now in a position of advantage because you have successfully navigated the complexities of podcast planning, production, and promotion through this guide. You have the knowledge, resources, and strategies required to create a podcast show that appeals to your target audience. You are set up for success now that you know how to produce interesting content, how to handle the technical aspects of recording and editing, and how to extend the reach of your podcast through successful marketing techniques.

Keep in mind that the charm of podcasting lies in its sincerity and the relationships it creates. So let your passion and expertise shine through in every episode you create. Let your podcast serve as a forum for knowledge exchange, deep discourse, and the development of a brand community.

CHAPTER 6

The Ongoing Content Creation Cycle for Podcasting: Idea Generation, Crafting Engaging Episodes, and Repurposing

For me, the best thing about long-form content creation is how easy it is to repurpose, repackage, and generate new content from a single video, blog, or podcast. I call this initial long-form content Genesis Content, because it can be used over and over again to create more ideas.

Let's look at how to continually create compelling podcast content and maximise its value across channels.

Step 1: Generate Smart Content Ideas

Consistently brainstorming fresh, engaging topics is an integral first step. Keep these ideas organised in a document, spreadsheet, or productivity tool. Do not let this list get to the end. My advice is to have at least 10 ideas lined up at all times.

Content ideation tactics include:

» Conduct detailed audience research into listeners' interests, burning questions, frustrations, and pain points via social listening, polls, interviews, and focus groups. Carefully align topics with what your specific audience wants to hear. As mentioned in Step 1 of Chapter 4.

» Closely analyse competitors and leading podcasts in your niche for inspiration on topics and angles, but always offer your own distinct take rather than replicating. I am a big believer in collaborating, not competing, so I'd recommend you engage with others in your niche to create content together.

» Stay on top of industry news, trends, data, and developments using tools like Google Alerts, Talkwalker, and Buzzsumo. Set up alerts for your niche keywords. Monitor hashtags. This is the key to becoming a key person of influence in your industry.

» Maintain an ongoing list of at least 20–30 potential guest experts who could provide insider insights and diverse perspectives on your podcast in different topic areas. Reach out systematically and add personal touches to your correspondence. Share why they are perfect for the show and how you can help them.

» Brainstorm a large pool of show segment ideas that could package insights from multiple episodes into compelling segment formats like "5 Key Lessons" or "Top Productivity Hacks". You can use generative AI to help you ideate and consider new viewpoints or content structures.

Step 2: Craft Truly Engaging Episodes

With your topics selected, carefully structure the content itself for maximum listener engagement.

» Make heavy use of stories, anecdotes, and examples to bring topics to life in a relatable, memorable way. Appeal to human interest and emotions, not just hard facts.

» Regularly incorporate interactive elements like Q&As with engaged listeners, contests, Twitter polls, or co-creating episode topics and segments with your audience.

» Frame guidance so each episode delivers tangible value for listeners, such as simplified frameworks, actionable tips, powerful quotables, helpful resources, or sheer entertainment.

» Maintain a clear and consistent release schedule, ideally with new episodes coming out on a predictable recurring day and time. This trains listeners to anticipate and engage with each new episode.

Step 3: Repurpose Content To Maximise Value

Be diligent in identifying creative opportunities to repurpose and repackage podcast content across other marketing channels. There have never been more tools and apps to help you make your content go further.

- » Transcribe full episodes into blog posts and articles. Expand on key sections and incorporate useful links. This widens reach and improves SEO.

- » Share short, compelling clips on social media to highlight engaging segments and quotable moments and promote the full episode.

- » Compile related episodes into 'best of' themed eBooks on popular topics that loyal listeners would find valuable as a downloadable resource.

- » Produce lead magnets and content based on the content from the podcast and make them available to your audience. These can be used for advertising campaigns too.

- » Segment longer interviews into a special highlights mini-series of short episodes with added commentary.

- » Savvy idea generation, thoughtful content structure, and creative repurposing together will continually fuel your content engine over the long term. Consistency truly compounds results!

Again, this is by no means a comprehensive list; the only restriction on how you can reuse content is your creativity. My philosophy is to take into account how each person prefers to learn and consume content. Consider repurposing content as the process of producing versions of your content that are user-friendly for your audience.

I know a podcaster whose social media followers and engagement are higher than those of her podcast audience, but all of her social media posts are drawn from the podcast. Evidently, her audience prefers quick social media posts to 45-minute audio podcasts.

This chapter has taken you through the ongoing content creation cycle for podcasting, underscoring the importance of constant ideation, crafting engaging episodes, and creative repurposing to get the most value from your content.

The journey begins with generating captivating content ideas that resonate with your audience and align with industry trends. The next step is transforming these ideas into engaging episodes filled with storytelling, interactivity, and tangible value.

But the cycle doesn't end here. By repurposing your podcast episodes, you can expand their reach across diverse platforms, taking your valuable content further. From transcripts to social media clips and eBooks, the potential for repurposing is boundless.

Remember, everyone consumes content differently. By catering to these varied preferences, you increase your chances of connecting with your audience in meaningful ways. It's all about creating, connecting, and amplifying.

As we wrap up this chapter, I encourage you to embrace this cycle as the heartbeat of your podcast strategy. Your voice has the power to create a real impact. It's time to amplify your reach and let your story be heard.

CHAPTER 7

Tackling the Major Podcasting Obstacles

While launching a podcast is immensely rewarding, all podcasters inevitably encounter obstacles along their journey.

The following challenges I've personally encountered, which I think the term "Imposter Syndrome" can best describe. My advice is to not let overwhelm and learning moments deter you. The advantages of maintaining consistency and continuing your education outweigh the disadvantages of succumbing to imposter syndrome. I like this quote to motivate me to advance in my career and in my personal life:

> **You don't have to be great to start, but you have to start to be great.**
>
> *Zig Ziglar*

So you are not alone, keep going! I hope this chapter helps guide you through these obstacles.

Next, we will methodically examine the most common challenges, as well as concrete solutions and constructive mindsets to persist through setbacks.

The Most Pervasive Challenges and Fears Plaguing New Podcasters

Let's extensively explore the typical obstacles and doubts podcasters face:

Fear of Public Speaking

A debilitating fear of public speaking or recording your voice affects approximately 73% of the population, according to studies.

For podcasting, repetitive exposure therapy is crucial. Start by recording short, 60 second practice episodes on unpressured topics. Progressively increase the episode length and listen back to get fully comfortable hearing your recorded voice. Improvement happens incrementally, so stay patient. This is why we edit, we can fix any moments you dislike. And you do not have to publish everything you record, if it doesn't meet your expectations, put it on the shelf

Tips:

1. **Practice**   Familiarise yourself with your material and rehearse your speech multiple times. This can help reduce anxiety and increase your confidence. Try practising in front of a mirror or recording yourself to identify areas for improvement.

2. **Breathing Exercises**   Deep, controlled breathing can help calm your nerves before and during your speech. Try inhaling for a count of four, holding for a count of four, and exhaling for a count of four.

3. **Positive Visualisation**   Imagine yourself delivering your speech confidently and successfully. Visualisation can help reduce anxiety and improve performance. Picture your audience reacting positively to your speech.

Overwhelming Technical Difficulties

Despite exponential advances in technology, over 50% of podcasters classify recording, editing, and publishing episodes as challenging. Begin with basic equipment like the tried-and-true ATR2100 mic (under $100) and free audio editing software like Audacity or GarageBand. Watch step-by-step video tutorials on proper setup, editing workflows, and publishing. Don't hesitate to outsource editing if needed. Upgrade equipment gradually over time.

Tips:

1. Preparation and Testing — Before recording, ensure all your equipment is working correctly. Test your microphone, headphones, and recording software. Make sure your recording environment is quiet and free of background noise.

2. Backup Equipment — Always have a backup plan in case your primary equipment fails. This could be an extra microphone, headphones, or a secondary recording device.

3. Outsourcing or Training — I use a system where I list all of the production tasks and assign each task either "love, hate, or takes too long". I look at each to establish if I can learn to do the slow tasks quicker or if I can outsource them with the "hate" tasks too.

Creative Doubts Around Consistent Content Generation

Without a system, coming up with engaging topic ideas week after week can seem daunting, leading to creative blocks. Schedule regular weekly or monthly brainstorming and topic planning sessions. Maintain an organised content calendar and an evolving list of at least 20–30 potential topics or guest recommendations. Actively gather audience questions. Follow news and trends related to your niche.

Tips:

1. **Content Planning**

   Develop a content calendar that outlines what topics you'll cover and when. This can help alleviate the stress of coming up with new ideas on the spot and ensure you have a consistent flow of content.

2. **Inspiration Sources**

   Regularly seek inspiration from various sources such as books, articles, other podcasts, conversations, and personal experiences. Keep a running list of potential topics or ideas that you can refer to when you're feeling stuck.

3. **Embrace Imperfection**

   Remember that not every piece of content has to be perfect. It's more important to share authentic and valuable content consistently. Don't let the pursuit of perfection hinder your creativity or consistency.

Discouraging Lack Of Listeners And Traction

Inconsistent traction and download numbers Falling short of expectations quickly deflates motivation. Remember that gradually building an audience inherently takes patience and consistency. Resist comparing yourself to successful, established podcasts. Instead, stay focused on delivering high-value content. Promote new episodes across all marketing channels. Traction accelerates over time.

Tips:

1

Analyse and Adjust

Use podcast analytics to understand what's working and what's not. If certain episodes have more downloads, try to understand why and replicate that success. Don't be afraid to experiment with different topics, formats, or promotional strategies.

2

Quality Over Quantity

Instead of focusing on the number of listeners, focus on the quality of your content. A smaller, engaged audience can be more valuable than a larger, disinterested one. Make each episode the best it can be, and the listeners will follow.

3

Networking & Collaboration

Reach out to other podcasters for collaborations or guest appearances. This can help you tap into their audience and bring new listeners to your podcast. Attend podcasting events or join online communities to connect with other podcasters and share experiences.

Maintaining Unwavering Consistency and Motivation

Persistence is essential to podcasting success. Beyond passion alone, the utilisation of these strategies will bolster consistency:

- ☐ Maintain an editorial calendar with future guest bookings, topics, and episode types scheduled out for the next 2-3 months to eliminate last-minute scrambles.

- ☐ Batch record multiple episodes in each studio session to build up an episode buffer as a cushion against unforeseen events derailing your cadence.

- ☐ Routinely celebrate progress and small milestones like releasing your 25th episode or reaching 1000 downloads rather than solely fixating on bigger end goals.

- ☐ Focus on improving versus your own past performance for a sense of progress rather than constantly comparing yourself negatively against others.

- ☐ Set manageable process-oriented goals like establishing a consistent release schedule or booking 5 guests rather than just big outcome goals like getting 10,000 downloads.

- ☐ Remember why you started the podcast in the first place. Who is it for, and how does it help them? This North Star can direct and guide you as you continue to create.

- ☐ Get help. As business leaders and entrepreneurs, it can feel like we have to take on the world alone. Content creation takes a lot of focus and resources to deliver high quality content. Reach out and find collaborators and support systems to make the effort less stressful.

Cultivating Constructive Mindsets Around Additional Challenges

Here are some more common obstacles podcasters encounter with healthy mindset shifts:

Technical Failures

→ **Problem:** Equipment malfunctions, files get corrupted or lost, or software crashes unexpectedly.

→ **Mindset:** Approach failures as valuable learning experiences rather than catastrophes. Troubleshoot issues before reacting emotionally. Backup everything.

Negative Feedback and Toxic Remarks

→ **Problem:** You receive hurtful criticism, toxic remarks, or demoralising reviews.

→ **Mindset:** Feedback helps you improve if it is constructive. Let toxic negativity go while taking genuine critique to heart.

Imposter Syndrome

→ **Problem:** You feel undeserving of positive feedback or success or are afraid of being exposed as a fraud.

→ **Mindset:** Remember that your knowledge and experience have inherent value to share. Stay humble and keep learning rather than dwelling on doubts.

Resource Limitations

➥ **Problem:** You have financial constraints, time limitations, or lack team support.

➥ **Mindset:** Be resourceful and maximise every current asset available, no matter how modest. Take it one step at a time.

With extensive solutions for common obstacles, any podcaster can overcome challenges on their journey to remarkable success. Stay committed, be resilient, and appreciate lessons learned, and your consistency will compound results over time!

Conclusion:
Begin Your Journey to Transform Your Business Through the Power of Podcasting

---

We've now extensively explored the immense yet attainable opportunities of podcasting and content creation to strengthen your brand, profoundly engage your audience, and grow a thriving business. While requiring commitment, the rewards make the journey profoundly worthwhile.

Remember The Platform And Influence Now Within Your Grasp

This guide has equipped you with the strategies and knowledge to shape your narrative on your terms, establish expertise around your unique experiences, forge deep human connections with your audience, and take control of your business's destiny.

Despite any obstacles faced, this potential for transformative growth is now within your grasp. Content creation allows you to share your authentic voice, wisdom, and perspective with the world. Podcasting presents a direct channel to inspire, educate, entertain, and build community with audiences eager to hear your message.

The Road Ahead

Recognise that building an audience and a thriving content channel is a gradual marathon requiring patience, experimentation, and resilience, not an overnight sprint chasing instant vanity metrics.

Stay determined when inevitably faced with challenges and setbacks. Let constructive feedback temper and guide you rather than discourage you. Find pride in celebrating incremental progress, not just crossing the finish line. The journey itself will shape you.

While the road ahead may seem long, you now hold all the blueprints within this guide to achieve remarkable success on your terms. I'm honoured to have been your guide across this terrain.

This Moment Marks Your Beginning

Today signifies when you courageously stepped forward to grow your business in exciting new ways through the power of podcasting. You pressed record on that first raw episode. You boldly launched your show into the world. You began sharing your expertise, stories, and vision.

Fulfil your potential to create an invaluable listening experience that deeply resonates with your audience while propelling your business into new realms of prosperity. You undeniably have this in you.

The time for action is right now. Your audience and community eagerly await to hear your one-of-a-kind voice, insights, and point of view.

I wish you the greatest success and fulfilment in creatively capturing hearts and minds on the adventure ahead. Your microphone awaits. Press record and begin!

Action Points:
Here is Your Roadmap for Success

———

You now have extensive knowledge and strategies to grow your business through podcasting. But that potential remains dormant until activated through consistent action.

Once you have followed the instructions in the book, you are prepared to begin. However, before continuing, make sure you have taken all necessary steps. I do not want your podcast to disappear into oblivion because you overlooked a crucial step.

If you are sure you have completed all the steps, now is the time to courageously start your podcasting journey.

Here is a roadmap to guide you:

1 Define Your Show Concept

- » Jot down initial podcast topic ideas and target audiences.

- » Refine the premise until it's clear, focused, and compelling.

- » Set goals like lead generation, brand building, etc. to inform strategies.

2 Map Out Your Content Calendar

- » Brainstorm specific topics or segments for the first 10–20 episodes.

- » Schedule guests and release dates using a content calendar.

- » Build an episode buffer to maintain consistency if issues arise.

3 Decide on the Right Format

» Will it be solo episodes, interviews, panels, or mixed?

» Select a format that best delivers value to your audience.

» Match the format to your brand, expertise, and style.

4 Get the Essentials to Start

» A USB mic like the Blue Yeti, headphones, and editing software are enough to begin.

» Refine production quality over time. Focus first on creating value for your audience.

5 Record a Pilot Episode

» Use your pilot to practise your flow, audio quality, editing, etc. before launch.

» Reflect on improvements to implement moving forward.

6 Launch Your Show!

» Once you've completed sufficient planning and preparation, it's go time!

» Present your best self and be content while keeping perfectionism at bay.

» Publishing that first episode is a massive milestone; celebrate!

7 **Engage Your Community**

» Spread the word across your website, email lists, social channels, etc.

» Don't be shy about asking for reviews, shares, and subscribers to grow your audience.

» Guest on aligned shows to gain access and cross-promote.

8 **Join The Thriving Podcast Community**

» For guidance and support every step of the way, join a podcast community and seek out events, meetups, and networks.

» Access actionable insights from myself and fellow podcasters.

Bio

Matt Cheney is a seasoned content creator, podcasting coach, and founder of Kult Media. An expert in inbound marketing strategies and content creation workflows, he uses his skills to help small businesses, marketing professionals, and creative entrepreneurs amplify their voices and make impactful first impressions.

In his debut book, "Inbound Amplification: Harnessing Podcasting for Business Growth", Matt brings together his expertise in personal branding for small businesses, content creation coaching, and podcast production. This holistic approach encapsulates his belief that everyone deserves the opportunity to be heard and that a strong, well-crafted message can create lasting impressions.

When he's not demystifying the podcasting world or developing innovative content strategies, Matt indulges his love for travelling and adventures in the wild, embodying a spirit of exploration that also drives his creative endeavours.

In the ever-evolving digital landscape, Matt's work exemplifies his commitment to helping others navigate the terrain, transforming podcasting from an intimidating venture into a dynamic tool for business growth.

Matt Cheney
Author and Coach

Dive into our useful links now

[1] https://contentmarketinginstitute.com/articles/b2b-power-content-marketing-research/

[2] https://www.linkedin.com/pulse/how-podcast-marketing-exploded-my-website-traf-fic-12-months-gillivan/

[3] https://www.nielsen.com/news-center/2022/nielsen-releases-third-podcasting-today-re-port/

[4] https://www.edisonresearch.com/the-infinite-dial-2022/

[5] https://www.pewresearch.org/journalism/2023/04/18/podcasts-as-a-source-of-news-and-information/

[6] https://www.edisonresearch.com/the-infinite-dial-2022/

[7] https://www.edisonresearch.com/the-infinite-dial-2022/

[8] https://discoverpods.com/podcast-statistics/

[9] https://www.pewresearch.org/journalism/2023/04/18/podcasts-as-a-source-of-news-and-information/

[10] https://contentmarketinginstitute.com/wp-content/uploads/2022/03/Tech_2022_Re-search-FINAL-3-17-22.pdf

[11] https://www.leadquizzes.com/?s=podcast

[12] https://rachelcorbett.com.au/blog/should-your-podcast-be-audio-or-video/

Inbound Amplification

How to harness podcasting
for business growth

Matt Cheney

www.ingramcontent.com/pod-product-compliance
Lightning Source LLC
LaVergne TN
LVHW051740050326
832903LV00023B/1024

Inbound Amplification

How to harness podcasting for business growth

Podcasting's meteoric rise presents an unprecedented opportunity for businesses to grow their brand, connect with customers, and drive real results.

In this comprehensive guide, podcasting expert Matt Cheney shares insider strategies and proven techniques to help you:

- ⇢ Launch your own podcast built around your brand and expertise.
- ⇢ Create compelling content that educates, entertains, and inspires your audience.
- ⇢ Integrate podcasting into your inbound marketing efforts for lead generation and sales.
- ⇢ Build personal connections and trust through intimate audio experiences.
- ⇢ Overcome common obstacles faced when starting and growing a podcast.

Whether you're brand new to podcasting or looking to take your show to the next level, this eBook will provide you with the roadmap and tools needed to engage your audience and succeed.

Unlock the immense power of podcasting for your small business with actionable advice from this industry veteran and host.

CLAIM YOUR COPY TODAY AND AMPLIFY YOUR VOICE!

ISBN 9798873752812

90000

9 798873 752812